100 PEOPLE WHO CHANGED AMERICA

With an Introduction by Newbery Author Russell Freedman!

SCHOLASTIC

D0104398

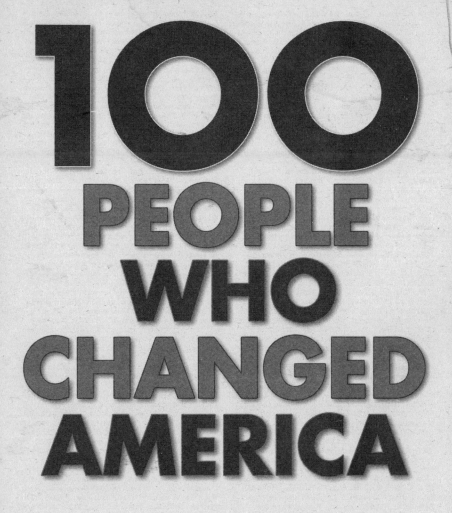

100 PEOPLE WHO CHANGED AMERICA

Introduction by Newbery Medal-winning
Author Russell Freedman

Scholastic Inc.
New York • Toronto • London • Auckland • Sydney
Mexico City • New Delhi • Hong Kong • Buenos Aires

ISBN 0-439-70999-7

Dear Reader,

What does it take to change America? What sort of courage is needed to step out of the crowd and truly make a difference?

Russell Freedman,
Newbery-winning author of
Lincoln: A Photobiography

Countless people have changed our country in many ways, but the 100 individuals included in this book have had an impact that demands special attention. Some were chosen for this list because they fought for social justice. Others led us through war. Still others have touched our lives through science or invention, through art, music, dance, or sports.

I've written about several of the people included here: Abraham Lincoln, the Wright brothers, Eleanor Roosevelt, and Babe Didrikson Zaharias, just to name a few. I chose to write about them because they inspired me with their words, their deeds, and often, their sheer guts. By exploring their life stories, I hoped to discover how they overcame obstacles, how they conquered their fears, and how they accomplished what they did. *For me, a biography needs to be a lot more than just a list of facts. It must be a window into a person's character.*

The photos and facts included on these pages are snapshot invitations for you to explore more about an individual's life. Which of these people do you wish you could meet? Who would you choose as a friend? You can use this book as a jumping-off point for your next writing assignment. Let the 100 pioneers on these pages inspire you to write a great biography of your very own.

I've found that people who accomplish something worthwhile are always guided by a dream. Nothing is more powerful than a dream. The men and women included here are proof that an individual with a dream can go forth and conquer the world.

Russell Freedman

Business & Law

Bill Gates
William Randolph Hearst
John Jay
Juliette Low
Thurgood Marshall
Sandra Day O'Connor
John D. Rockefeller, Jr.
Muriel "Mickie" Siebert
Madam C. J. Walker
Oprah Winfrey

Bill Gates

Born: October 28, 1955

Born William Henry Gates III

As cofounder and chairman of Microsoft Corporation and the creator of Microsoft Windows, he helped bring America into the computer age. He began programming computers at the age of 13.

Fast facts:

- One of the wealthiest men in the world
- Family calls him "Trey" because he's William Gates III
- Started the Bill and Melinda Gates Foundation, which funds educational scholarships and fights to stop AIDS and other diseases in poorer countries

William Randolph Hearst

Born: April 29, 1863
Died: August 14, 1951

After inheriting a San Francisco newspaper his father had won gambling, William Randolph Hearst was the first person to create a media empire. By the time he died, he owned more than 20 newspapers, 18 magazines, and several radio and movie companies.

Fast facts:

- Hearst's name became synonymous with "yellow journalism," a way of reporting that doesn't always stick to the facts
- History shows that the editorials and sensational reporting in Hearst newspapers helped drive America into the war with Spain in 1898
- Assembled one of the world's greatest private art collections at his mansion in San Simeon, California

John Jay

Born: December 12, 1745
Died: May 17, 1829

A lawyer and New York state representative, he would become one of the most important founders of our country. As the first Chief Justice of the Supreme Court, appointed by George Washington, he became a strong advocate of the Constitution.

Fast facts:

- Wrote the controversial Jay's Treaty that allowed British ships to inspect American ships suspected of carrying supplies to France, Britain's enemy
- Contributed five essays to the Federalist Papers, which called for the approval of the Constitution

Juliette Low

Born: October 31, 1860
Died: January 17, 1927

Known as "Daisy"

She founded the Girl Scouts of the U.S.A. to bring girls of all backgrounds into the outdoors and give them the opportunity to develop independence. She encouraged girls to prepare not only for traditional homemaking, but for roles as professional women, too.

Fast facts:

- Decided to start the Girl Scouts of the U.S.A. after meeting Sir Robert Baden-Powell, creator of the Boy Scouts and Girl Guides in England
- The Girl Scouts included disabled youngsters at a time when they were excluded from many other activities
- Liked to take in stray animals and was fond of exotic birds

Thurgood Marshall

Born: July 2, 1908
Died: January 24, 1993

As a lawyer, he argued and won the landmark *Brown v. Board of Education* case ending "separate, but equal" schools and was one of the greatest fighters for civil rights. As the first African American Supreme Court justice, he continued to work for racial equality and fairness.

Fast facts:

- Went to Lincoln University in Pennsylvania with poet Langston Hughes and musician Cab Calloway
- Was denied admission to the University of Maryland Law School because he was African American

Sandra Day O'Connor

Born: March 26, 1930

At a time when few women worked outside the home, she became a lawyer. She had a hard time, however, finding a law firm that would hire a woman. Eventually, she would work her way up to become an assistant attorney general, a trial judge, and the first woman to serve on the Supreme Court.

Fast facts:

- Grew up in Texas and originally thought of becoming a cattle rancher
- The Senate voted unanimously to put O'Connor on the Supreme Court

John D. Rockefeller, Jr.

Born: January 29, 1874
Died: May 11, 1960

The son of America's first billionaire, he believed that his enormous wealth carried with it great responsibility. He gave more than 500 million dollars to charities and other worthy causes and is particularly well known for buying land to save the wilderness and build national parks.

≡Fast facts:

- ☉ Established the Rockefeller Foundation to "promote the well-being of mankind throughout the world"

- ☉ Sponsored Rockefeller Center in New York City, founded the University of Chicago, and restored Colonial Williamsburg

Muriel "Mickie" Siebert

Born: September 11, 1932

"The First Woman of Finance"

She arrived in New York in 1954 with $500 and no job. In just a few years, she would become the first woman to own and operate a brokerage firm and to own a seat on the New York Stock Exchange (NYSE). In 1977, she became New York's banking superintendent.

≡Fast facts:

- ☉ On her 30th anniversary on the NYSE, her dog, Monster Girl, joined Muriel as she rang the closing bell

Madam C. J. Walker

Born: December 23, 1867
Died: May 25, 1919

Born Sarah Breedlove McWilliams Walker

At a time when both women and African Americans faced enormous prejudices, she founded the Madam C. J. Walker Manufacturing Company to sell hair care products. Her hugely successful business would make her one of the first female self-made millionaires.

Fast facts:

⊙ *Invented the conditioning treatment to straighten hair*

⊙ *The "C. J." in her name stands for her husband's name, Charles Joseph*

⊙ *Was a generous donor to black charities, including the NAACP; also purchased Frederick Douglass's home and turned it into a museum*

Oprah Winfrey

Born: January 29, 1954

She's made book clubs popular across the country, encouraged Americans to eat better and exercise, and made it all right for people to talk about their experiences and their feelings. Her extraordinarily successful talk show has won 39 Emmy Awards and has informed our nation for almost 20 years.

Fast facts:

⊙ *Was named after Orpah from the Book of Ruth in the Bible; the name was misspelled as Oprah on her birth certificate*

⊙ *Chairman of her production company, HARPO Productions, which is OPRAH spelled backward*

⊙ *Oscar-nominated for her role in the movie* The Color Purple

Inventors & Innovators

Benjamin Banneker
Alexander Graham Bell
Clarence Birdseye
Nolan Bushnell
Willis Haviland Carrier
George Washington Carver
Walt Disney
Thomas Alva Edison
Henry Ford
Benjamin Franklin
Milton Hershey
Steven Jobs
Maya Lin
J. Robert Oppenheimer
Elisha Graves Otis
Noah Webster
Eli Whitney
Frank Lloyd Wright
Orville and Wilbur Wright

Benjamin Banneker

Born: November 9, 1731
Died: October 9, 1806

The child of slaves, he taught himself science and math. As a boy, he took a watch apart, studied it, and then made his own. As an adult, he was an inventor, farmer, mathematician, and astronomer who figured out how to predict both solar and lunar eclipses. *Benjamin Banneker's Almanac*, published between 1791 and 1802, was a top seller throughout the early United States.

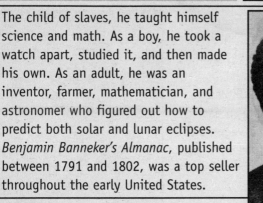

Fast facts:

- Was a land surveyor for the area now known as the District of Columbia
- Image was featured on a postage stamp in 1980

Alexander Graham Bell

Born: March 3, 1847
Died: August 2, 1922

Imagine a world without telephones! At the age of 27, Alexander Graham Bell successfully communicated to his assistant in a different room over his "electrical speech machine." He went on to found the first Bell Telephone Company and launched a whole new American industry.

Fast facts:

- Invented the first crude metal detector and tried using it to find an assassin's bullet after President Garfield had been shot (But he didn't find the slug)
- Decibel (dB) is a measure of sound named for Bell

11

Clarence Birdseye

Born: December 9, 1886
Died: October 8, 1956

After watching Eskimos freeze fish in barrels of Arctic water, he invented the Quick Freeze Machine. The freshly frozen foods he distributed through his Birdseye products allowed people to eat fresh-tasting fruits and vegetables instead of canned or pickled ones.

Fast facts:

- *Food freezing dates back as early as 1626, but Birdseye's packaging made it accessible to everyone*
- *Was willing to eat anything—claims to have tried chipmunks, whale, beaver tail, even the front half of a skunk!*

Nolan Bushnell

Born: February 5, 1943

Nolan Bushnell has always loved games and, as the founder of Atari Inc., he is the creator of *Pong*, the first home video game. In addition, he helped to popularize video arcades where kids can go to challenge and entertain themselves.

Fast facts:

- *Created his first game,* Computer Space, *in 1971 in his daughter's bedroom*
- *Started the popular restaurant and entertainment chain, Chuck E. Cheese*
- *Played tournament chess in college*

Willis Haviland Carrier

Born: November 26, 1876
Died: October 9, 1950

His invention of air-conditioning made everyday life more comfortable for people all across the United States. It also revolutionized the workplace, because people could be more productive and cooler in the summer months.

≡Fast facts:

◉ *His first customers for air-conditioning were Madison Square Garden and the U.S. Senate and House chambers*

◉ *The first air-conditioned home was in Minneapolis, Minnesota, and was called a "weather maker."*

George Washington Carver

Born: 1865 (exact date unknown; during Civil War)
Died: January 5, 1943

Born just as African Americans were freed from slavery, this educator, researcher, and botanist created one of the most popular foods in America today—peanut butter! In fact, he developed more than 325 products from the peanut, including shampoo.

≡Fast facts:

◉ *Known as "the plant doctor" as a child*

◉ *Also created more than 100 products from sweet potatoes*

INVENTORS & INNOVATORS

Walt Disney

Born: December 5, 1901
Died: December 15, 1966

Born Walter Elias Disney

Mickey Mouse. Goofy. Disney World. It's impossible to imagine a world without the magical contributions to animation and children's entertainment of Walt Disney. In his lifetime, he won more than 32 Academy Awards. Today, the company he founded is still entertaining children around the world.

≡*Fast facts:*

⊙ *Released the first cartoon with synchronized sound,* Steamboat Willie, *in 1928*

⊙ *Produced the first-ever animated feature film in the U.S.A.,* Snow White and the Seven Dwarfs

Thomas Alva Edison

Born: February 11, 1847
Died: October 18, 1931

"To invent you need a good imagination and a pile of junk," he once wrote. Edison patented more than 1,093 inventions, including the phonograph and the lightbulb. His discoveries also led to the creation of motion pictures. Without him, our modern lives would look very different.

≡*Fast facts:*

⊙ *His first patent was for an electric vote checker*

⊙ *Edison made the lightbulb last longer so it could be sold and used by the public*

⊙ *Started Edison Electric Light Company in New York*

Henry Ford

Born: July 30, 1863
Died: April 7, 1947

In 1908, his Ford Motor Company developed the first moving automobile assembly line. This allowed him to make cars more quickly—and sell them cheaply. Soon everyone was "hitting the highways."

Fast facts:

- Patented the first plastic-bodied car (using soybean products to make the plastic!)
- Mobilized his factories for the war effort and produced bombers, Jeeps, and tanks for World War II

Benjamin Franklin

Born: January 17, 1706
Died: April 17, 1790

Writer, printer, publisher, scientist, diplomat, revolutionary, inventor—he succeeded at everything he did. When he went to France as an ambassador to get help for the American Revolution, his simple, rustic manners and creative imagination made him a symbol of all that the new country stood for.

Fast facts:

- His Poor Richard's Almanac introduced popular sayings like "A penny saved is a penny earned"
- Some of his inventions include the lightning rod, bifocals, and the Franklin stove
- Picture is featured on the $100 bill

Milton Hershey

Born: September 13, 1857
Died: October 13, 1945

The first candy shop he opened failed, but after he learned how to add fresh milk to caramels, he became a successful manufacturer. Soon he was also making chocolates and the first mass-produced candy. The rest is delicious history!

Fast facts:

- Attended school through fourth grade and then went to work as a printer's apprentice
- Built the town of Hershey, Pennsylvania, where streetlamps are in the shape of Hershey's Kisses
- When he and his wife could not have children of their own, he opened the 10,000-acre Milton Hershey School for children in social and financial need

Steven Jobs

Born: February 24, 1955

The first computers were expensive and enormous—for use only by scientists at universities. However, Steven Jobs changed all that when he was only 21. Working out of his garage with his childhood friend Stephen Wozniak, he created the Apple Computer and launched the personal computer revolution.

Fast facts:

- In 1986, cofounded and currently runs Academy Award-winning Pixar animation studio, which produced popular movies like Toy Story, Monsters, Inc., and Finding Nemo

Maya Lin

The Vietnam Memorial she designed is both simple and moving. On a long black slab of marble that descends into the ground are engraved more than 50,000 names of the soldiers who died in the war. Lin, a Chinese American architect, designed what is now known as "The Wall" located in Washington, D.C., when she was only 21.

⦿Fast facts:

- ⦿ Her design for the Vietnam Memorial was chosen from 1,400 entries in a national contest
- ⦿ Is inspired by many different sources, from Japanese gardens to Indian earthen mounds

J. Robert Oppenheimer

Born: April 22, 1904
Died: February 18, 1967

"The Father of the Atomic Bomb"

A brilliant physicist, he led the Manhattan Project, the secret World War II effort to create the first atomic bomb. After the bombs destroyed Hiroshima and Nagasaki in Japan, however, he would spend the rest of his life trying to prevent the spread of nuclear weapons, first as Chairman of the U.S. Atomic Energy Commission and later through his many writings and speeches.

⦿Fast facts:

- ⦿ When he was a child, he collected minerals and became a member of the New York Mineralogical Club
- ⦿ Was dismissed as Chairman of the U.S. Atomic Energy Commission after wanting to stop countries from using nuclear weapons

INVENTORS & INNOVATORS

17

Elisha Graves Otis

Born: August 3, 1811
Died: April 8, 1861

He was working in a factory in New York when he invented a safety mechanism for lifting heavy loads. This simple elevator brake changed the way buildings would look forever. Skyscrapers began shooting up toward the clouds, and the race was on to build the world's tallest buildings.

Fast facts:

- At the 1854 Crystal Palace Exhibition, demonstrated his device to the public for the first time, riding an elevator to great heights and then asking his assistant to chop the rope with an ax—proving the elevator was safe and would not fall
- The Otis name can be found inside most modern elevators

Noah Webster

Born: October 16, 1758
Died: April 15, 1843

He didn't like school when he was a child because the books were all in English—not "American"! As a schoolteacher himself, in 1806, he finished and published the first American dictionary and established a new homegrown version of the English language.

Fast facts:

- The first dictionary included new American words like "skunk" and "squash" and Americanized the spellings of many English words
- The first dictionary had approximately 70,000 words and took more than 20 years to research

Eli Whitney

Born: December 18, 1765
Died: January 8, 1825

His famous cotton gin built in 1793 turned cotton from a money-losing crop into a money-maker. As more cotton was produced, more slaves were needed to produce it. After the cotton gin, the yield of raw cotton doubled each decade.

Fast facts:

- ◉ *Although his father died when he was only four, Whitney's uncles Eli and Philos (who ran an armory and also were inventors) influenced his development*

- ◉ *Also invented a way to manufacture muskets by machine*

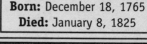

Frank Lloyd Wright

Born: June 8, 1867
Died: April 9, 1959

This experimental architect built a house around a waterfall, designed a spiral museum, and showed Americans how to think outside the box. Of his more than 1,141 total projects, only 532 were actually constructed, but many of them are still in use today.

Fast facts:

- ◉ *Credited his love of landscape to his early years growing up in the Wisconsin countryside*

- ◉ *Designed churches, schools, bridges, homes (including Fallingwater, the house built around a waterfall) and museums (including the Guggenheim Museum in New York City)*

INVENTORS & INNOVATORS

Orville Wright

Born: April 16, 1867
Died: May 30, 1912

Wilbur Wright

Born: August 19, 1871
Died: January 30, 1948

On December 17, 1903, these two brothers proved that man could do the unthinkable—fly. Wilbur made the first attempt in the *Wright Flyer* at Kitty Hawk in North Carolina. But he stalled on takeoff. Three days later, Orville became the first human to fly, traveling 120 feet in 12 seconds.

Orville Wright

Fast facts:

- *Started the Wright Cycle Co. in 1883 where they manufactured their own bicycles*
- *First learned about flight by watching birds and then by reading books about flying— even though they eventually proved that the books had been wrong!*
- *By the fall of 1905, Wilbur made a flight circling a field that lasted 39 minutes for a distance of 24 ½ miles*

Wilbur Wright

Leaders &
Social Change

Jane Addams

Susan B. Anthony

Mary McLeod Bethune

Jimmy Carter

Cesar Chavez

Shirley Chisholm

Frederick Douglass

Thomas Jefferson

Helen Keller

John F. Kennedy

Martin Luther King, Jr.

Abraham Lincoln

Wilma Mankiller

Rosa Parks

Alice Paul

Pocohontas

Ronald Reagan

Eleanor Roosevelt

Franklin Delano Roosevelt

Theodore Roosevelt

Gloria Steinem

Sojourner Truth

Harriet Tubman

George Washington

LEADERS & SOCIAL CHANGE

Jane Addams

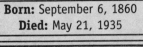

Born: September 6, 1860
Died: May 21, 1935

She devoted her life to helping people less fortunate than herself. From creating the first public playground in Chicago to the founding of Hull House, America's first community center for poor families, she was tireless in her efforts to end the sufferings of the poor.

≣Fast facts:

⊙ Fought for child labor laws, workers' rights, and women's right to vote

⊙ Awarded the Nobel Peace Prize in 1931

Susan B. Anthony

Born: February 15, 1820
Died: March 13, 1906

She never got to vote in an election, but because of her pioneering work, women have that right today. Ignoring all kinds of abuse and opposition, she toured the country trying to convince people that women deserved equal rights.

≣Fast facts:

⊙ Best friend was Elizabeth Cady Stanton, who wrote some of the most important documents in the Women's Rights Movement

⊙ Helped form the antislavery group, The Women's Loyal National League, collecting more than 300,000 signatures to end slavery

⊙ In 1872, Anthony tried to vote and was promptly arrested, jailed, and fined $100—but she never paid it

Mary McLeod Bethune

Born: July 10, 1875
Died: May 18, 1955

She thought that nothing was more important—or more powerful—than a good education. After working as a teacher and a missionary, she founded one of the first schools and hospitals for African Americans. "We must gain full equality in education...and full equality in the abundance of life," she said.

Fast facts:

- Wanted to be a missionary in Africa, but decided to stay in America where she became a teacher, visiting prisons, serving the homeless, and counseling the poor
- In 1985, she was honored with a postage stamp and a statue in a Washington, D.C., park
- Founded the National Council of Negro Women

Jimmy Carter

Born: October 1, 1924

Born James Earl Carter, Jr.

He's built houses with Habitat for Humanity. He's flown around the world to ensure fair elections. When he was the thirty-ninth president, he helped make a historic peace agreement between Egypt and Israel. For this dedication to human rights, he was awarded the Nobel Peace Prize in 2002.

Fast facts:

- First U.S. president born in a hospital
- Before he was president, he was a peanut farmer and businessman
- The first presidential candidate from the Deep South to be elected since the Civil War

Cesar Chavez

Born: March 31, 1927
Died: April 23, 1993

During the Great Depression, his family lost everything and joined the thousands of migrant workers who toiled in the fields for little pay and few benefits. In 1962, he founded the National Farm Workers Association to fight for the dignity and recognition of all farmworkers.

Fast facts:

- *Held national boycotts and refused to eat (fasted) as a form of protest against bad working conditions and poor wages for migrant workers*
- *In 1988, held his longest fast (36 days) against supermarkets that sold California grapes to protest the use of pesticides*
- *In 2002, he was honored by the United States Postal Service with a stamp*

Shirley Chisholm

Born: November 30, 1924

Not only was she the first African American woman elected to Congress— she had the first all-female staff when she went to Washington. During seven terms as a New York representative, she worked hard to equalize women's rights. She is the cofounder of the National Organization for Women (NOW).

Fast facts:

- *Is a founding member of the Congressional Black Caucus and the National Women's Political Caucus*
- *Ran for the Democratic Presidential nomination in 1972*

Frederick Douglass

Born: circa 1818
Died: February 20, 1895

Born Frederick Augustus Washington Bailey

When he was a slave, he would trade his food to neighborhood boys so they'd teach him to read and write. When he finally escaped slavery, the stories he wrote about his experiences became a powerful force of change. Writer, speaker, journalist—he lived to see his people free.

Fast facts:

- ☉ *Was an advisor to President Abraham Lincoln*
- ☉ *Wrote three different autobiographies during his lifetime, including the best-selling* The Narrative of the Life of Frederick Douglass: An American Slave

Thomas Jefferson

Born: April 13, 1743
Died: July 4, 1826

A strong believer in religious freedom and what he called "the natural rights of man," he served the country he helped found. He was governor of Virginia, secretary of state, vice president, and the second president of the United States But he will always be most famous as the author of the Declaration of Independence.

Fast facts:

- ☉ *Was responsible for the Louisiana Purchase, a deal to buy land that doubled the size of the United States*
- ☉ *Called the "father of archaeology" because he discovered a superior technique of digging*
- ☉ *Appears on the nickel and the $2 bill*

Helen Keller

Born: June 27, 1880
Died: June 1, 1968

Nothing held this girl back. Even though she was deaf and blind, she graduated from Radcliffe College with honors, traveled worldwide, and was awarded the Presidential Medal of Freedom in 1964. During her lifetime, she was a role model for the disabled.

Fast facts:

⊙ Met 12 U.S. presidents

⊙ Good friends with Alexander Graham Bell, Mark Twain, and Franklin Roosevelt

⊙ Known for saying "Life is either a daring adventure or nothing."

John F. Kennedy

Born: May 29, 1917
Died: November 22, 1963

"Ask not what your country can do for you, ask what you can do for your country," he urged in his 1961 inaugural address as the thirty-fifth president. Although he was assassinated in 1963, during his term of office, he created the Peace Corps, launched Project Apollo to put a man on the moon, and guided the country through the terrifying days of the Cuban Missile Crisis.

Fast facts:

⊙ Was the first Roman Catholic president

⊙ Served as president for only 1,037 days

⊙ Donated his presidential salary to charities

Martin Luther King, Jr.

Born: January 15, 1929
Died: April 4, 1968

He didn't just have a dream, he had a mission—to change the world peacefully. The nonviolent social action he led as part of the Civil Rights Movement forced people everywhere to see the evils of racism. He was the youngest person ever to win the Nobel Peace Prize.

≡Fast facts:

- ⊙ *Was born Michael Luther King, Jr. but changed his name to Martin*
- ⊙ *Assassinated on April 4, 1968*
- ⊙ *The third Monday of every January is designated Martin Luther King Day, a national holiday*

Abraham Lincoln

Born: February 12, 1809
Died: April 15, 1865

Born in a log cabin, this country lawyer became one of America's greatest presidents. As the sixteenth president, he led America through its darkest days during the Civil War and issued the Emancipation Proclamation, which called for an end to slavery.

≡Fast facts:

- ⊙ *Is the tallest president at 6'4"*
- ⊙ *11-year-old Grace Bedell wrote a letter asking him to grow a beard—and he did*
- ⊙ *Assassinated by John Wilkes Booth on April 14, 1865 at Ford's Theatre in Washington, D.C.*

Wilma Mankiller

Born: November 18, 1945

When she was little, her family, part of the Cherokee Nation, was "relocated" from Oklahoma to California by the Bureau of Indian Affairs. Eventually, she moved back to Oklahoma, her ancestral home, and became the first woman to lead a Native American tribe in modern times.

Fast facts:

⊙ *Her family name, "Mankiller," is believed to be an old military title given to the person in charge of protecting the village*

⊙ *Was seriously injured in a car collision in the late 1970s; she nearly lost a leg and had 17 operations*

⊙ *Received the Presidential Medal of Freedom in 1998*

Rosa Parks

Born: February 4, 1913

Born Rosa Louise McCauley

On December 1, 1955, in Montgomery, Alabama, Rosa Parks was arrested because she refused to give up her seat on a bus to a white man. This act of courage started a new chapter in the Civil Rights Movement, and showed how one person could help change the way people think.

Fast facts:

⊙ *Was a seamstress before she became famous*

⊙ *Honored with a Congressional Gold Medal in 1999*

⊙ *Martin Luther King, Jr. led the Montgomery Bus Boycott after her arrest*

Alice Paul

Born: January 11, 1885
Died: July 9, 1977

She was willing to do almost anything to help women get the right to vote. She picketed the White House. She went on hunger strikes. Many times, she was arrested and put in solitary confinement. Finally, she achieved her goal in 1920 with the 19th Amendment to the Constitution, which gave women the right to vote.

≣Fast facts:

- ◌ *Authored the Equal Rights Amendment*
- ◌ *Formed the National Women's Party (NWP)*

Pocohontas

Born: circa 1595
Died: 1617

Without this Native American's help, the first American colony in Jamestown, Virginia, would have failed. She brought food to the colonists and helped secure peace between them and the local Native Americans. She died of smallpox at 21, but her son, Thomas, became an important leader in the colony.

≣Fast facts:

- ◌ *Pocohantas is a Powhatan tribe nickname meaning "playful" or "spoiled child"; her real name was Matoaka*
- ◌ *In 1612, Pocohontas was held hostage, but then met and married a colonist, John Rolfe*
- ◌ *After learning English, she was baptized as Rebecca Rolfe*

Ronald Reagan

Born: February 6, 1911
Died: June 5, 2004

A former movie actor, he was known as the "Great Communicator" because of his almost effortless ability to connect with the American people. As the fortieth president, he influenced the end of the Cold War and Communism.

🗏Fast facts:

- ⊙ Was a lifeguard for seven years and is said to have saved more than 77 people from drowning
- ⊙ Costarred with a chimpanzee in the movie Bedtime for Bonzo
- ⊙ Was the oldest elected president at 69 years and 349 days and served two terms

Eleanor Roosevelt

Born: October 11, 1884
Died: November 7, 1962

Married to Franklin Delano Roosevelt, she used her platform as First Lady to fight for human rights around the world. She gave lectures, radio broadcasts, and had a daily newspaper column, "My Day." After her husband's death, she helped found UNICEF and was a spokesperson for the United Nations.

🗏Fast facts:

- ⊙ When the King and Queen of England came to the White House, she served hot dogs—picnic-style!
- ⊙ Established the United Nations Universal Declaration of Human Rights, which has been translated into more languages than any document in the world

Franklin Delano Roosevelt

Born: January 30, 1882
Died: April 12, 1945

"The only thing we have to fear is fear itself," the thirty-second president said as he led the country through the Great Depression and World War II. He served longer than any other president (16 years) and created social reforms with his New Deal that continue to protect the old, the poor, and the disabled.

Fast facts:

- First president to regularly address the public with radio broadcasts
- Suffered from polio and used a wheelchair—but only two public photos show him in it
- Built a swimming pool and a movie theater inside the White House

Theodore Roosevelt

Born: October 27, 1858
Died: January 6, 1919

He was a military leader, a bigger-than-life adventurer, and a diplomat. But it was his vision to create a system of national parks and forests for which he will be most remembered. During his presidency, he preserved more than 230 million acres of American wilderness.

Fast facts:

- First president to ride in a car, fly in a plane, dive in a submarine, and travel outside the United States (during the building of the Panama Canal)
- The teddy bear is named after him because he spared a baby bear cub on a hunting trip
- Awarded Nobel Peace Prize and Congressional Medal of Honor

Gloria Steinem

Born: March 25, 1934

Her favorite book as a girl was *Little Women*. She liked the story of a group of girls who looked out for themselves. The founder of *Ms. Magazine* and spokeswoman for the feminist movement, she gave a voice to women who wanted the same rights and equality as men.

Fast facts:

⊙ *In the 1970s, she helped to found the National Women's Political Caucus, the Women's Action Alliance, and the Coalition of Labor Union Women*

⊙ *Is the author of numerous best-selling books, including* Outrageous Acts and Everyday Rebellions *and* Revolution from Within: A Book of Self-Esteem

Sojourner Truth

Born: circa 1797
Died: November 26, 1883

Born Isabella Baumfree or Bomefree

After she escaped from slavery, she was one of the earliest and most passionate abolitionists (people who worked to abolish slavery). She lectured widely on the cruelties she'd experienced and is best known for her "Ain't I a Woman?" speech, given at the Women's Rights Convention of 1851.

Fast facts:

⊙ *Raised food and clothing contributions for black regiments during the Civil War, and met Abraham Lincoln at the White House in 1864*

⊙ *In 1997, NASA's Mars Pathfinder robotic rover was named* Sojourner *in her honor*

Harriet Tubman

Born: circa 1820
Died: March 10, 1913

Born Araminta Ross

Born a slave around 1820, she risked her life to go back and lead slaves to freedom on the Underground Railroad. In all, she made more than 18 trips and freed more than 300 slaves, including her own parents. "I never ran my train off the track, and I never lost a passenger," she said.

⌇Fast facts:

- ⊙ *Trying to save another slave from punishment when she was only 15, Tubman got hit in the head with a weight—an injury that gave her blackouts for the rest of her life*
- ⊙ *Also worked as a cook, nurse, and spy in the Civil War*

George Washington

Born: February 22, 1732
Died: December 16, 1799

He was commander in chief of the army in the American Revolution and the first elected president of the United States. As the "father" of our country his name and likeness appear on everything from the one dollar bill to monuments and schools. Our nation's capital is named after him.

⌇Fast facts:

- ⊙ *His first job? Land surveyor*
- ⊙ *His teeth were so bad that he only had one real one remaining in his mouth when he was inaugurated as president; his sets of false teeth were made of everything from hippo ivory to other human teeth—but no wooden ones!*

LEADERS & SOCIAL CHANGE

33

Music & Arts

Maya Angelou
Chuck Berry
Margaret Bourke-White
Emily Dickinson
W.E.B. DuBois
Ella Fitzgerald
Theodor Geisel
Martha Graham
D.W. Griffith
Jim Henson
Langston Hughes
Toni Morrison
"Jelly Roll" Morton
Georgia O'Keeffe
Elvis Presley
Norman Rockwell
Steven Spielberg
Mark Twain
Andy Warhol
Walt Whitman

Maya Angelou

Born: April 4, 1928

Born Marguerite Johnson

Her moving story about her childhood, *I Know Why the Caged Bird Sings*, gave a new voice to the African American experience and offered people everywhere an inspiring message of hope. She grew up in a segregated world but became an award-winning actress, an acclaimed poet, and a best-selling writer.

≡Fast facts:

- ⊙ Is fluent in English, French, Spanish, Italian, Arabic, and West African Fanti
- ⊙ The second inaugural poet, she read an original poem at President Bill Clinton's inauguration in 1993
- ⊙ Received more than 50 honorary degrees from colleges and universities around the United States

Chuck Berry

Born: October 18, 1926

John Lennon of the Beatles called Chuck Berry "the inventor of rock and roll." Berry's songs like "Johnny B. Goode" and "Maybellene," brought a new sound and beat to American music. He is known as one of the greatest songwriters of the rock-and-roll era.

≡Fast facts:

- ⊙ A clip of his hit song "Johnny B. Goode" played in the spacecraft *Voyager I* in 1977
- ⊙ Was inducted into the Rock and Roll Hall of Fame in 1986

MUSIC & ARTS

Margaret Bourke-White

Born: June 14, 1904
Died: August 27, 1971

As the first female photojournalist for *Life* magazine, she documented America during the Great Depression of the 1930s. Margaret was also the first woman war correspondent. She sent home pictures from the battles of World War II and the Nazi concentration camps. Her photos not only recorded history— they made it.

Fast facts:

- Last person to photograph Gandhi before he was killed
- Suffered from Parkinson's disease

Emily Dickinson

Born: December 10, 1830
Died: May 15, 1886

During her life she published fewer than ten poems, but she wrote more than 1,800. After her sister and niece brought out collections of her verse in the early twentieth century, however, generations of writers would be inspired by her exciting experimentations of language, punctuation, and poetic form.

Fast facts:

- Assembled her poems in packets bound with needle and thread and hid them in closets and trunks
- Lived in almost total isolation from the outside world by the 1860s

W.E.B. DuBois

Born: February 23, 1868
Died: August 27, 1963

Born William Edward Burghardt DuBois

Throughout his life, DuBois fought against racism. He worked as a journalist, and was the first African American to receive a Ph.D. from Harvard. A cofounder of the National Association for the Advancement of Colored People (NAACP), he championed reforms that would improve the lives of all African Americans.

≡Fast facts:

⊙ *Writer and intellectual whose many books include* The Souls of Black Folk

⊙ *Moved to Africa in the early 1960s and died there just one day before Martin Luther King, Jr.'s famous March on Washington*

Ella Fitzgerald

Born: April 25, 1917
Died: June 15, 1996

Known as the First Lady of Song, she was the most popular jazz singer in America for more than 50 years. By the time she died, Ella had recorded more than 200 albums, won 13 Grammy Awards, and was able to imitate any instrument in the orchestra with her voice.

≡Fast facts:

⊙ *Big break: her name was pulled in a drawing at the Apollo Theater's Amateur Night, and she wowed the crowd*

⊙ *First big hit was "A-Tisket, A-Tasket," recorded when she was only 21 years old*

Theodor Geisel

Born: March 2, 1904
Died: September 24, 1991

"Dr. Seuss"

He made it fun for kids to learn to read! From *The Cat in the Hat* and *Green Eggs and Ham* to *How the Grinch Stole Christmas!* his "Dr. Seuss" books have been the ones children read first on their own. More than 200 million of his books have been sold in more than 15 different languages worldwide.

Fast facts:

⊙ While studying at Oxford, the woman who was to become his wife saw him doodle on a page and told him he should be an artist

⊙ Added the word "Dr." to his name because his father always wanted a doctor in the family

Martha Graham

Born: May 11, 1894
Died: April 1, 1991

"The Mother of Modern Dance"

She wasn't the first dancer to throw away her ballet shoes, but her bold, passionate way of moving has influenced most of today's modern dancers. Martha created more than 180 dances and founded the Martha Graham School for Contemporary Dance in New York. She was awarded the Presidential Medal of Freedom and the National Medal of Arts.

Fast facts:

⊙ First choreographer to regularly employ African American and Asian American dancers

⊙ Continued to dance and perform until she was older than 70

D. W. Griffith

Born: January 22, 1875
Died: July 21, 1948

Born David Lewelyn Wark Griffith

Before *The Lord of the Rings* or *Star Wars*, there were the epic films of D. W. Griffith, one of the very first movie directors. He introduced close-ups, crosscutting, and film-editing techniques in movies such as *The Birth of a Nation* and *Intolerance*. Between 1907 and 1914 he made more than 450 movies.

Fast facts:

- Helped develop many of the techniques that are still used when shooting movies today
- Cofounder (with Charlie Chaplin, Douglas Fairbanks, and Mary Pickford) of United Artists, the first major independent film company

Jim Henson

Born: September 24, 1936
Died: May 16, 1990

Born James Maury Henson

Without him there would have been no Big Bird, no Ernie, no Kermit the Frog. The most famous puppeteer in history, his warmhearted and inventive creations have entertained—and educated—both young and old through television and feature films. With *Sesame Street*, characters such as Oscar the Grouch and Cookie Monster became household names.

Fast facts:

- The word "Muppet" comes from a combination of the words "puppet" and "marionette"
- Established the Jim Henson Foundation to develop the art of puppetry in the United States

MUSIC & ARTS

Langston Hughes

Born: February 1, 1902
Died: May 22, 1967

Born James Langston Hughes

Hughes is known for his leadership in the Harlem Renaissance, a period of artistic and social expression in the early 1920s. Hailed as the "Negro Poet Laureate," he inspired a generation of artists, musicians, and writers to express their African American heritage in their work.

Fast facts:

⊙ *Some of his earliest jobs were as a cook, a busboy, and a seaman traveling to Africa and Europe*

⊙ *Wrote a famous column in the country's most influential African American newspaper,* The Chicago Defender

Toni Morrison

Born: February 18, 1931

Born Chloe Anthony Wofford

Toni Morrison says that it is her job as a writer to give a voice to people who had never had a chance to tell their stories. Audiences around the world were captivated by books such as *Beloved* and *Song of Solomon*, which told of the challenges and triumphs of the African American experience.

Fast facts:

⊙ *First African American and eighth woman to receive the Nobel Prize in Literature*

⊙ *Was 39 when she wrote her first novel,* The Bluest Eye

"Jelly Roll" Morton

Born: October 20, 1890
Died: July 10, 1941

Born Ferdinand Joseph Lamothe

His business card read "Originator of JAZZ—STOMP—SWING" and most musicians would agree. He was a pianist and bandleader whose early twentieth-century "ragtime" music would influence the development of jazz and big-band music.

Fast facts:

- Had a diamond stud in his front tooth
- Also worked as gambler, pool shark, and comedian

Georgia O'Keeffe

Born: November 15, 1887
Died: March 6, 1986

Georgia O'Keeffe's breathtaking paintings of flowers and desert scenes made her both successful and famous. She showed the world a different side of the American West. She once wrote, "I could say things with color and shapes that I couldn't say any other way."

Fast facts:

- An area called Ghost Ranch in New Mexico is the inspiration for many of her paintings
- Married photographer Alfred Stieglitz, who organized many of her art exhibits

MUSIC & ARTS

41

Elvis Presley

Born: January 8, 1935
Died: August 16, 1977

"The King of Rock and Roll"

The first rock-and-roll superstar. He sold more than one billion records, had 149 songs on Billboard's "Hot 100" Pop Chart, starred in 33 movies, and is in the Rock and Roll, Country Music, and Gospel Music Halls of Fame.

Fast facts:

- Got his first guitar when he was 11
- First breakthrough hit was "That's All Right"
- His home, Graceland, in Memphis, Tennessee, is now a museum; fans gather there for Elvis Week each August

Norman Rockwell

Born: February 3, 1894
Died: November 8, 1978

Every week he painted a scene of American life that appeared on the cover of the popular magazine, *The Saturday Evening Post*. These realistic pictures were loved by people all over America who recognized themselves in his everyday scenes.

Fast facts:

- Hired as an art director for Boys' Life magazine—when he was still a teenager!
- Painted The Problem We All Live With, which appeared in Look magazine in 1964, and shows Ruby Bridges's historic walk into a newly desegregated school
- Later in his life, Rockwell painted pictures illustrating some of America's most important issues including civil rights, poverty, and space exploration

Steven Spielberg

Born: December 18, 1946

"I dream for a living," filmmaker Steven Spielberg once said. With *Close Encounters of the Third Kind* and *ET*, he brought aliens to the movies. With *Schindler's List* and *Saving Private Ryan*, he made us confront the terrible realities of war. His films have won numerous Academy Awards.

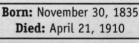

Fast facts:

- ⊙ *Directed some of the most financially successful (and favorite) films of all time, including E.T., Jaws, Jurassic Park, and Raiders of the Lost Ark*
- ⊙ *Founding partner of DreamWorks SKG, Hollywood's first new studio in 75 years*

Mark Twain

Born: November 30, 1835
Died: April 21, 1910

Born Samuel Langhorne Clemens

His story of an escaped slave and a runaway boy on the Mississippi River, *The Adventures of Huckleberry Finn*, is ranked as one of America's greatest novels. His books, such as *The Adventures of Tom Sawyer*, are filled with adventure and humor, and his many stories have delighted readers of all ages for more than a hundred years.

Fast facts:

- ⊙ *Twain was also a steamboat pilot and gold prospector*
- ⊙ *The name "Mark Twain" is a pun on the term that refers to a riverboat depth for safe water*

MUSIC & ARTS

Andy Warhol

Born: August 6, 1928
Died: February 22, 1987

Born Andrew Warhola

The inventor of "pop art" became famous in the 1960s for his paintings of Campbell's soup cans and celebrities. A painter and filmmaker who lived in New York City, he brought popular culture to the world of art. In words that are often repeated, he once said, "In the future, everyone will be world-famous for fifteen minutes."

Fast facts:

- His images were often silk-screened, which allowed them to be repeated endlessly
- Published a popular magazine called Interview

Walt Whitman

Born: May 31, 1819
Died: March 26, 1892

In his poems, Walt Whitman celebrated everything about the world around him—from the Brooklyn Bridge to his own thoughts and sensations. His book of poetry, *Leaves of Grass*, continues to be an inspiration to poets, artists, and musicians.

Fast facts:

- Although he had no formal education, Whitman often attended opera and studied great books in New York's libraries
- His poem "When Lilacs Last in the Dooryard Bloom'd" is about President Abraham Lincoln's funeral procession

New Frontiers

Neil Armstrong
Clara Barton
Rachel Carson
William Clark
Amelia Earhart
Albert Einstein
Robert Goddard
Mae Jemison
Meriwether Lewis
Charles Lindbergh
Sally Ride
Sacajawea
Jonas Salk
James Watson

Neil Armstrong

Born: August 5, 1930

A former naval aviator and test pilot, he was chosen to be the Commander of *Apollo 11* and led the first manned space mission to the moon in 1969. For ten years, thousands of scientists had worked toward this moment. His words when he set foot on the lunar surface ("That's one small step for man, one giant leap for mankind") paid tribute to their achievement.

⸬Fast facts:
- ☉ *Flew more than 200 aircraft including jets, rockets, helicopters, and gliders*
- ☉ *The first moon footprint was the size of Armstrong's space boot, 13" x 6"*

Clara Barton

Born: December 25, 1821
Died: April 12, 1932

A nurse from Massachusetts, she founded the American Red Cross in 1881. She then recruited women to gather medical supplies for the front lines, where she witnessed some of the bloodiest battles of the Civil War. She said of the soldiers, "What could I do but go with them, or work for them and my country?"

⸬Fast facts:
- ☉ *President Lincoln put Barton, known as the Angel of the Battlefield, in charge of locating missing men from the Union army—and she found thousands*
- ☉ *Convinced America to sign the Geneva Agreement in 1882, which provides rules for the fair treatment of those wounded or killed during war*

Rachel Carson

Born: May 27, 1907
Died: April 14, 1964

Rachel Carson was a marine biologist and naturalist. Upset by the widespread use of synthetic chemical pesticides after World War II, she wrote a book in 1962, *Silent Spring*. It exposed the dark side of science by showing the dangerous effects of pesticides. When it was published, the chemical companies called her "a hysterical woman," unfit to write such a book. Today, she is considered the mother of modern environmentalism.

Fast facts:

- Her first job was writing radio scripts for the U.S. Bureau of Fisheries during the Depression
- In Silent Spring, *Carson introduced the world to "ecosystems," a word that describes the interaction between living things and their environment*

William Clark

Born: August 1, 1770
Died: September 1, 1838

Trekking over 8,000 miles in two years, he and his partner Meriwether Lewis were the first Europeans to explore, map, and describe the Western territory of America. A noted geographer and map-maker, the route Clark charted would open up the country for the pioneers.

Fast facts:

- A large black Newfoundland dog named Seaman accompanied the men on the trip
- Carried with them 193 pounds of "portable soup," a paste made of beef, eggs, and vegetables

NEW FRONTIERS

Amelia Earhart

Born: July 24, 1897
Died: July 2, 1937

"Women must try to do things as men have tried," she wrote. She was the first woman to make solo flights across the Atlantic and Pacific Oceans, and the United States. In 1937, her plane disappeared on route to Howland Island (halfway between Hawaii and Australia) during an attempted flight around the world, and her disappearance remains an unsolved mystery to this day

⌕Fast facts:

- ◉ On December 28, 1920, Amelia took her first plane ride. She said, "By the time I had got two or three hundred feet off the ground, I knew I had to fly."
- ◉ Took Eleanor Roosevelt on a nighttime flight over Washington, D.C.

Albert Einstein

Born: March 14, 1879
Died: April 18, 1955

He didn't speak until he was four and didn't do very well in school, but in 1905 his theory of relativity would change the way people viewed space, time, and matter. In 1921, he was awarded the Nobel Prize in Physics.

⌕Fast facts:

- ◉ Historians call 1905 Einstein's "Miracle Year": In one year, he originated four major physics theories while still holding down a full-time job at the patent office
- ◉ Favorite hobbies included sailing, painting, and playing the violin; if he had not been a scientist, Einstein said he probably would have been a musician

Robert Goddard

Born: October 10, 1882
Died: August 10, 1945

Inspired by H. G. Wells's science fiction classic *The War of the Worlds*, this physics professor from Massachusetts dared to believe in rocket travel when no one else did. When he built the first liquid fuel-propelled rockets, he paved the way for the modern space age.

Fast facts:

- Launched his first rocket in a cabbage field
- Charles Lindbergh helped Goddard get an important grant so he could continue with his research in Roswell, New Mexico

Mae Jemison

Born: October 17, 1956

Dr. Mae Jemison blasted into orbit aboard the space shuttle *Endeavour* on September 12, 1992. She was the first woman of color to go into space. Now she is the founder and president of two technology companies. Space flight was just the beginning for this dynamic woman.

Fast facts:

- While in medical school, she traveled to Cuba, Kenya, and Thailand to offer people medical care
- Worked in the West Africa Peace Corps as a medical officer
- Founded The Earth We Share™ (TEWS), an annual international science camp where students from around the world work together to solve current global dilemmas

NEW FRONTIERS

Meriwether Lewis

Born: August 18, 1774
Died: October 11, 1809

With his lifelong interests in botany and zoology and his military service, he was chosen by President Thomas Jefferson to lead an expedition across the new country documenting its plants and animals. After his three-year trip with partner William Clark, he became the new governor of the Louisiana Territory.

Fast facts:

- *Thomas Jefferson thought Lewis and Clark might find erupting volcanoes, mountains of salt, and wooly mammoths out west*

- *Members of the exploring team ate approximately 6 pounds of meat each day—the equivalent of 24 hamburgers!*

Charles Lindbergh

Born: February 14, 1902
Died: August 26, 1974

One of the first aviators, Lindbergh loved the sky. He was a stunt pilot, flew combat missions in World War II, and learned to skydive in later life. He is most famous for achieving the first nonstop solo flight across the Atlantic Ocean.

Fast facts:

- *His wife, Anne Morrow Lindbergh, became his copilot and navigator on expeditions around the world*

- *The kidnapping of his youngest son, Charles, Jr., in 1932, is considered by some to be the "crime of the century" because of Lindbergh's worldwide fame*

- *Won the Pulitzer Prize for The Spirit of St. Louis, a book about his nonstop solo flight*

NEW FRONTIERS

Sally Ride

Born: May 26, 1951

She applied to NASA's astronaut program on an impulse and became the first American woman in space and the youngest American ever to circle Earth. After accomplishing her own out-of-this-world achievements, she started Imaginary Lines, a program to support girls in science and math.

≡Fast facts:

⊙ In high school, she dreamed of becoming a professional tennis player

⊙ Is a member of the Astronaut Hall of Fame

Sacajawea

Born: circa 1787
Died: reported as December 20, 1812

She led Lewis and Clark across America to the Pacific Coast, her infant baby strapped to her back. Along the way she served as a translator and diplomat with the Native American tribes they met. "A woman with a party of men is a token of peace," explained Clark.

≡Fast facts:

⊙ Was born in the Shoshone tribe but then kidnapped to the Hidatsa tribe, where she was named Sacajawea, meaning "bird woman"

⊙ Said to have rescued valuable tools and instruments and, most important, Lewis and Clark's extensive journals when a boat tipped over

⊙ Appears on the U.S. dollar coin

Jonas Salk

Born: October 28, 1914
Died: June 23, 1995

In 1952, Jonas Salk, a doctor at the Virus Research Lab at the University of Pittsburgh introduced a vaccine to prevent polio—a disease that could cripple and kill people. Today, polio vaccines are still given around the world to fight this deadly disease.

Fast facts:

- Born to Russian-Jewish immigrants, he was the first person in his family to attend college
- Did not patent his polio vaccine because he said he did not want to profit from it—he wanted to make it as widely available as possible
- Spent his final years in the lab seeking a vaccine for the AIDS virus

James Watson

Born: April 6, 1928

With his partner Francis Crick, he unlocked the structure of DNA, the molecule out of which all living matter is made. Their discoveries would revolutionize the study of biology, genetics, and medicine. Watson and Crick were awarded the Nobel Prize in Medicine in 1962.

Fast facts:

- Amateur bird-watcher since he was a young boy
- Entered college at age 15 and got a degree in zoology
- Led the Human Genome Project at the National Institutes of Health, a project that identified the location and function of all human genes

NEW FRONTIERS

Sports

Muhammad Ali
Michael Jordan
Jackie Joyner-Kersee
Billie Jean King
Bruce Lee
Jesse Owens
Jackie Robinson
Wilma Rudolph
Babe Ruth
Jim Thorpe
Tiger Woods
Babe Didrikson Zaharias

Muhammad Ali

Born: January 17, 1942

Born Cassius Marcellus Clay, Jr.

When Ali was 12, someone stole his bike. Ali said he wanted to "whup" whoever did it. A cop told him he'd better learn to box first, so he did. He won the world heavyweight title in 1964 and became the greatest boxer of the twentieth century.

Fast facts:

- *Was known as much for his big mouth as for his boxing; nicknamed the "Louisville Lip" early in his career*
- *Described his own boxing style: "Float like a butterfly, sting like a bee"*

Michael Jordan

Born: February 17, 1963

With five Most Valuable Player awards, six NBA Championships with the Chicago Bulls, and two Olympic gold medals to his credit, the 6' 6" tall Jordan is one of the greatest stars of basketball history. He's been on the cover of *Sports Illustrated* over fifty times, more than any other athlete!

Fast facts:

- *Played in 1,072 games for a total of 41,011 minutes and finished his career with 32,292 points*
- *Called "his Airness" in reference to the hang time attained during his slam dunks*

SPORTS

Jackie Joyner-Kersee

Born: March 3, 1962

Born Jacqueline Joyner

This African American Olympian has been called one of the best all-around athletes in the world. Others simply refer to her as "Wonder Woman" because of her gold medal-winning performance in the heptathlon, a seven-event track and field competition that lasts two grueling days.

Fast facts:

⊙ *Was named after first lady Jacqueline Kennedy because her grandmother always said, "Someday this girl will be the first lady of something"*

⊙ *Started the Jackie Joyner-Kersee Boys & Girls Club in East St. Louis, Illinois, so she could give back to her community*

Billie Jean King

Born: November 22, 1943

Born Billie Jean Moffitt

She was the first female athlete to speak openly about sexual inequality in sports. In 1973, King defeated former Wimbledon Champion Bobby Riggs in the "Battle of the Sexes" tennis match, proving that women players were just as exciting to watch as men.

Fast facts:

⊙ *First female athlete to win more than $100,000 in prize money in a single season*

⊙ *Won 71 singles titles and 20 Wimbledon titles (including singles, doubles, and mixed doubles)*

⊙ *Founded the Women's Tennis Association (WTA)*

SPORTS

Bruce Lee

Born: November 27, 1940
Died: July 20, 1973

Born Lee Hsiao Lung

As a kid, Lee was a loner who always got into fights. He took up kung fu to discipline himself, eventually becoming the first martial arts superstar. His blockbuster movie, *Enter the Dragon*, introduced martial arts to the western world.

Fast facts:

- The son of a famous Chinese opera singer, he was born in San Francisco and grew up in Hong Kong
- Was famous for his two-finger push-ups and his one-inch punch (a punch through an object at a close distance)

Jesse Owens

Born: September 12, 1913
Died: March 31, 1980

Born James Cleveland Owens

The African American track-and-field legend won four gold medals at the 1936 Olympics in Berlin. Before the competitions began, Adolf Hitler predicted that white men would win all the events. Owens proved him wrong.

Fast facts:

- Got the name Jesse from a teacher who misunderstood when he said his name was J.C. (for James Cleveland)
- Because African Americans were not awarded athletic scholarships, he had to work his way through Ohio State University

Jackie Robinson

Born: January 31, 1919
Died: October 24, 1972

Born Jack Roosevelt Robinson

In 1947, Robinson signed a contract with the Brooklyn Dodgers, integrating the team to become the first African American to play for Major League Baseball. Despite death threats, players who taunted and attacked him, and fans who mocked him, he persevered with his dramatic style of play and showed the world that baseball was bigger than bigotry.

Fast facts:

- In college, was a lettered varsity athlete in basketball, football, track, and baseball
- Stole 197 bases in his professional career with the Brooklyn Dodgers—19 of them at home plate

Wilma Rudolph

Born: June 23, 1940
Died: November 12, 1994

"The Black Gazelle"

As a child in Tennessee, she was forced to wear a brace on her "bad leg" after a bout of polio. As an adult, through hard work and determination, this track superstar beat the odds to become the first woman to win three gold medals at a single Olympics. This took place in Rome, Italy, in 1960.

Fast facts:

- In addition to polio, she suffered from double pneumonia and scarlet fever
- As a sprinter, was undefeated in all of her high school track meets

SPORTS

57

Babe Ruth

Born: February 6, 1895
Died: August 16, 1948

Born George Herman Ruth, Jr.

Sultan of Swat and Home Run King are just two of the many nicknames he earned in his amazing baseball career. He gained the most fame as a New York Yankee, hitting 60 home runs in 1927, a record that stood until 1961. Ruth led the American League in home runs 12 times and holds the lifetime slugging average at .690.

Fast facts:

- ⊙ *Credited with the invention of the modern baseball bat*
- ⊙ *Threw and batted left-handed, but wrote right-handed*

Jim Thorpe

Born: May 28, 1887*
Died: March 28, 1953

Born Jacobus Franciscus Thorpe

Born on an Oklahoma reservation, his Native American name "Bright Path" seemed to predict his future. By the end of his career, he had won Olympic gold medals in both the pentathlon and decathlon events and had become known as the most powerful all-around athlete in the history of sports.

Fast facts:

- ⊙ *Three-time hall-of-famer in football, track and field, and the Olympic games*
- ⊙ *Founded, and was the first president of, what is now the National Football League (NFL)*

Although he has no official birth certificate, this is the official date declared by his estate

SPORTS

58

Tiger Woods

Born: December 30, 1975

Born Eldrick Woods

This child prodigy had his first hole-in-one by age eight. By 28, he had won 53 tournaments, including 8 major PGA Tour events, giving him one of the most successful careers in golfing history—with many more years still to go.

≡Fast facts:

- ☉ *Played nine holes of golf at age three, was featured in* Golf Digest *by age five*
- ☉ *Won three consecutive junior amateur titles and three amateur titles before turning professional*
- ☉ *Typically wears a red shirt on the final day of any golf tournament*

Babe Didrikson Zaharias

Born: June 26, 1911
Died: September 27, 1956

Born Mildred Ella Didrikson

America's first female golf superstar, Babe was successful in just about every other sport as well—including basketball, baseball, tennis, diving, volleyball, bowling, skating, cycling... even boxing. And somewhere she found time to win an Olympic gold medal in track and field in the 1932 Olympic games in Los Angeles, CA.

≡Fast facts:

- ☉ *Got the nickname "Babe" (after Babe Ruth) when she hit five home runs in a baseball game*
- ☉ *Was one of the founders of the Ladies Professional Golf Association (LPGA)*

SPORTS

Bio POP Quiz

Ready to test your Bio-Q? Can you answer these 15 questions (based on facts and figures found inside the book) without peeking back at the 100 profiles? Test your friends, too!

Answers on page 62

1. **Famous females first! Match each woman to her famous accomplishment.**

   a. Mae Jemison
   b. Muriel "Mickie" Siebert
   c. Wilma Rudolph
   d. Sandra Day O'Connor
   e. Toni Morrison

   1. First woman Supreme Court Justice
   2. First American woman to win three gold medals at a single Olympics
   3. First woman on stock exchange
   4. First African American Nobel Prize winner
   5. First woman of color in space

2. **What famous Native American person traveled with Lewis and Clark on their journey west?**

   a. Shoshone
   b. Sacajawea
   c. Pocahontas
   d. Hidatsa

3. **Who painted pictures of Campbell's soup cans?**

   a. Georgia O'Keeffe
   b. Frank Lloyd Wright
   c. Jim Henson
   d. Andy Warhol

4. **Who had a NASA Mars Pathfinder's robotic rover named after her?**

   a. Mary McLeod Bethune
   b. Pocohontas
   c. Sojourner Truth
   d. Sacajawea

5. Match that inventor! Who worked with which important object?

a. Eli Whitney   **1.** Telephone
b. Alexander Graham Bell   **2.** Air conditioner
c. Willis Carrier   **3.** Personal computer
d. Steve Jobs   **4.** Cotton gin

6. Who fought for women's rights?

a. Susan B. Anthony   **c.** Gloria Steinem
b. Alice Paul   **d.** All of the above

7. Whose business card read "Originator of JAZZ—STOMP—SWING?"

a. Ella Fitzgerald   **c.** "Jelly Roll" Morton
b. Thurgood Marshall   **d.** Chuck Berry

8. Put these presidents in chronological order by birth.

a. Ronald Reagan   **e.** George Washington
b. Theodore Roosevelt   **f.** Jimmy Carter
c. Abraham Lincoln   **g.** Thomas Jefferson
d. Franklin Delano Roosevelt   **h.** John F. Kennedy

9. What "sweet" man opened a school for children?

a. John D. Rockefeller, Jr.   **c.** Jim Henson
b. Milton Hershey   **d.** Cesar Chavez

10. How long was the Wright Brothers' first successful flight?

a. 39 minutes   **c.** 12 minutes
b. 5 seconds   **d.** 12 seconds

11. Match the famous person's nickname to his or her better-known name.

a. Ella Fitzgerald	1. The Sultan of Swat
b. Babe Ruth	2. The Mother of Modern Dance
c. Elvis Presley	3. The Angel of the Battlefield
d. Clara Barton	4. The King of Rock and Roll
e. Martha Graham	5. First Lady of Song

12. Where did Rosa Parks make history?

a. School picket line	c. Labor union
b. On a bus	d. Suffragette rally

13. Who invented the first fuel-powered rocket?

a. Robert Goddard	c. James Watson
b. Neil Armstrong	d. Albert Einstein

14. Who appears on the dollar coin?

a. George Washington	c. Pocohontas holding a bushel of corn
b. Sacajawea	d. Thomas Jefferson and his quill pen

15. Say what? Who originated these famous lines?

a. "A penny saved is a penny earned."	1. Neil Armstrong
b. "The only thing we have to fear is fear itself."	2. Benjamin Franklin
c. "That's one step for man, one giant leap for mankind."	3. Amelia Earhart
d. "Women must try to do things as men have tried."	4. Franklin Delano Roosevelt

Biography Writing Tips

1. Choose a person you admire or want to know more about.

2. Brainstorm good questions about the person you picked. What makes this person interesting to you? What are some of their greatest achievements?

3. Make a simple list of facts you want to include in your biography. Some things to consider:

   - Name, date, and place of birth
   - Education
   - Occupation
   - Major achievements
   - Family
   - Fun facts and quotes

4. Research and read as much as you can about your subject. Much of your research will probably be from secondary resources like almanacs, encyclopedias, and other biographies. Whenever possible, use primary resources like diaries, letters, and newspaper accounts to get firsthand information.

5. Take notes as you read on either note cards or paper. At the top of each note card indicate the source of your information. Later this will help you create a thorough bibliography. For more information on how to write a bibliography go to *http://helponenglish.homestead.com/Citation.html*

6. When you write your biography:

   - **Organize your information.** Biographies are usually written in chronological order. A timeline may be helpful.

   - **Be accurate.** Make sure you have at least three sources for your information.

   - **Get your readers' attention.** Include exciting personal details and quotes.

Resources

Check your school and local library for books and articles on the person you picked. Other places to look for information:

http://www.s9.com/biography/

http://www.historychannel.com

http://www.greatwomen.org/home.php

http://www.americanpresidents.org/

http://www.genealogy.com/bio/bio_top_dm.html

Index